PENGUIN BOOKS

The Gifts of Reading

Robert Macfarlane is the author of prizewinning and bestselling books about nature, place and people, including *Mountains of the Mind*, *The Wild Places*, *The Old Ways*, *Landmarks* and *The Lost Words* (with Jackie Morris). His work has been translated into many languages, and adapted for film, television, radio, stage and music. In 2017 he was awarded the E. M. Forster Prize For Literature by the American Academy of Arts and Letters. Robert Macfarlane is a Fellow of Emmanuel College, Cambridge, and *Underland* will be published in May 2019.

The Gifts of Reading

ROBERT MACFARLANE

PENGUIN BOOKS

PENGUIN BOOKS

UK | USA | Canada | Ireland | Australia
India | New Zealand | South Africa

Penguin Books is part of the Penguin Random House group of companies
whose addresses can be found at global.penguinrandomhouse.com.

First published 2016
This edition published 2017

007

Text design by Claire Mason
Typeset by Penguin Books
Printed and bound in Great Britain by Clays Ltd, Elcograf S.p.A.

A CIP catalogue record for this book is available from the British Library

ISBN: 978-0-241-97831-3

Penguin Random House is committed to a
sustainable future for our business, our readers
and our planet. This book is made from Forest
Stewardship Council® certified paper.

To Don

The Gifts of Reading

THIS STORY, like so many stories, begins with a gift. The gift, like so many gifts, was a book – and the book was given to me by a man called Don, with whom I became friends in Beijing during the autumn and winter of 2000. Don and I were working as English literature teachers in a university on the west side of the city, third ring-road out. Our students were mostly the sons and daughters of high-cadre officials: if you mentioned Tibet or Taiwan, thirty faces dipped to their desks. We taught our syllabus from a fat crimson-jacketed anthology of English literature that reframed literary history, Chinese Communist Party style. Literature was functional – and its function was the advancement of the Maoist project. Wordsworth the revolutionary was included, but not Wordsworth the late-life conservative. Oscar Wilde starred as socialist but not as aesthete. Ezra Pound didn't make the cut, for obvious reasons. Thomas Hood's 'The Song of the Shirt' was the most important Victorian poem.

Teaching with The Big Red Book, as we nicknamed it, was hard work. It was easy to forget that literature might be there to thrill, perplex or amaze, rather than only to instruct. What kept me honest was Don. Don turned sixty that year. He was from San Francisco. He was tall, just starting to stoop. He dressed Kerouac-style: black jeans, black leather jackets, white T-shirts. Pebble glasses, short grey hair standing up in spikes. Small, sharp, wonky teeth, which you saw a lot of because

Don talked so much and laughed so much.
Fast, rat-a-tat questions-and-answers, or long
think-pieces, but without ever making you
feel like he was taking more than his fair share
of airtime. I guess it was the speed he spoke
at — he packed in several words a second.

Don was from a blue-collar background in
California, and had met poetry at the City
Lights Bookstore in his early twenties. It had
changed his life. He'd heard Ginsberg read.
He'd hung out with Ferlinghetti. He worked
night school and then part-time at a state
college to get a degree in literature as a mature
student. But eventually he couldn't afford to
live in California and teach the texts he loved,
so he'd switched to Beijing where
accommodation came with the job, and the
basics were cheap. I don't think I've ever
known anyone with a higher-voltage passion

for books than Don. Literature *wired* him. When Don read, he crackled.

In the days, Don and I did our best with The Big Red Book and the cadre children. In the evenings, we drank beer laced with formaldehyde, and talked writing. Don introduced me to dozens of authors of whom I cannot now imagine being innocent, among them Ed Abbey, Annie Dillard and Gary Snyder. We shared a love of classical Chinese poetry (Li Bai, Tu Fu), especially in translations by Pound and by David Hinton. Although foreign books were difficult to come by in Beijing at that time, and expensive if you could find them, and although Don didn't have much money, he pressed volume after volume on to me, including his copy of Ferlinghetti's *A Coney Island of the Mind*, with its lit-up monochrome cover. 'Have it,' he told me, 'you'll love it, you *need* to read it, you keep it.'

One day Don didn't show up for his classes. He'd been mugged the night before. He was found in an alley in a pool of blood with a half-brick next to him and his wallet gone. I cut class and went straight to see him. His head had been shaved and there was a linen bandage swaddling half his skull, stained with iodine. But he was smiling, and there was a book open by his bed, and he wanted me to read him Snyder's poem 'Riprap' out loud:

> Lay down these words
> Before your mind like rocks.
> placed solid, by hands . . .

I left Beijing after two semesters, and came back to Cambridge to start a PhD in Victorian

literature. Don and I wrote often, sometimes
by email, mostly by airmail. I missed his
intensity – the seminar rooms of Cambridge
felt prim and flat in comparison. We arranged
that he'd come to England the next summer for
a couple of weeks. I couldn't wait to see him.

The visit didn't go to plan. I was struggling
with my doctorate, anxious, pressed for time.
Don wanted to talk, walk and read *all* day.
I needed to study. He wanted to explore the
bookshops of Cambridge – G. David's, the
Haunted Bookshop, both tucked away on
opposite sides of a medieval cemetery. So did
I. But I also felt obliged to put in hours in the
University Library, where I was tracking down
obscure texts from the 1860s in the huge
leather-backed folder that constituted the
catalogue in that pre-digitized era. After five
days I suggested that Don head up to

Edinburgh for a trip on his own. It was an astonishing city, I said, unmissable, the Paris of the North, etc. I researched bus times for him. I knew I was trying to move him on. I didn't know he knew I was trying to move him on.

On the seventh morning I heard Don get up early and walk around the house. The front door closed. I guessed he was heading to the market. I went to the kitchen to make coffee. There was a neatly wrapped present on the table, with a card. He'd gone to Edinburgh, hadn't wanted to wake us before leaving. I felt a quick punch of guilt. He'd loved his stay with us, had left a few small tokens of thanks. The present on the table was a copy of Snyder's *Mountains and Rivers Without End*. I walked into the other room. There was another present there, propped up against a lamp: a CD of West Coast jazz. And then in the room in which I worked, on my desk, was the third and last of his presents. It was a paperback copy of a book by Patrick Leigh Fermor that Don and I had talked about once in Beijing, drawn to it by our shared love of walking (which Don mostly did in cities, and I mostly did in mountains). Its title was *A Time of Gifts*.

*

If you have never read *A Time of Gifts*, may I urgently suggest that you buy a copy as soon as possible, or better still ask someone to give you one as a present? Together with the two books that follow it — *Between the Woods and the Water* (1986) and *The Broken Road* (2013) — it tells the story of Leigh Fermor's legendary walk from the Hook of Holland to Constantinople in the early 1930s, started when he was just eighteen, and constituting what is

fondly known by Leigh Fermor's many
modern admirers as 'the longest gap year
in history'.

Leigh Fermor came up with his plan at
'about lamplighting time at the end of a wet
November day' in Mayfair in 1933. Fatigued
by his London life and its boozy repetitions,
he was suddenly seized by the idea of walking
across an entire continent, from Christendom
to Islam, passing as he did so through the
cultures, tongues and countries of Europe. His
aim on setting out was to live like a 'pilgrim'
or 'errant scholar': to sleep in ditches and hay
barns, and 'only consort with peasants and
tramps'. But being who he was – a handsome
and charming young man with a few good
connections to start him off – he ended up
strolling from castle to castle, playing
hopschloss across Germany, Hungary and the

Carpathians, sipping Tokay from cut-glass goblets, and smoking yard-long pipes with archdukes and earls. For a year and a half, he was an aristocratic supertramp, enjoying hospitality along the way, making his rakish progress through the doomed world of Mitteleuropa, snatching scenes from a snow-globe – just before it was shattered by the worst war in history.

A Time of Gifts is filled with gifts and acts of giving – it is a book, we might say, that is rich with generosity. Among its gifts is the gift of time: Leigh Fermor did not publish it until 1977, forty-four years after beginning his walk, and a result of that long and thoughtful delay is a narrative voice which possesses both the joyful wonder of youth, and the wisdom and perspective of later age. And among those wisdoms is its reflection on the nature of gift:

what it might mean to give without expectation of recompense, and what types of kindness might stand outside the reciprocal binds of the cash economy.

This fascination with gift expresses itself also in Leigh Fermor's famously ornate style, profusely tendrilled as it is with trope and allusion. Almost everything in his prose leads to something else (path to path, culture to culture, word to word) and this abundance of connection is itself a kind of offering up or giving away. You feel, as a reader, passionately – perhaps even at times oppressively – hosted: *Read this! Look here! Listen to that! Walk this way!* His style is gratuitous in the best sense of that word: 'given free of charge; undertaken without necessity or obligation'.

One of the first things Leigh Fermor is given in *A Time of Gifts* is a book: the first volume of the Loeb edition of Horace. His

mother ('she was an enormous reader') bought
it for him as a farewell present, and on its
flyleaf she wrote the prose translation of an
exquisite short poem by Petronius, which
could hardly have been more appropriate as
a valediction to her son:

Leave thy home, O youth, and seek out alien
shores . . . Yield not to misfortune: the far-off
Danube shall know thee, the cold North-wind
and the untroubled kingdom of Canopus
and the men who gaze on the new birth of
Phoebus or upon his setting

*

The journey of *A Time of Gifts* is set going by the
gift of a book – and it is a book that has in turn set
going many journeys. The edition of *A Time of*

Gifts that Don gave me that day in Cambridge had as its cover a beautiful painting by John Craxton, commissioned specially for the book, and clearly alluding to Petronius's poem. It shows a young man standing on snowy high ground, looking eastwards to where the sun is rising orange over icy mountains, from which runs a mighty river. Black crows fly stark against white trees: there is a sense of huge possibility to the day ahead and to the land beyond.

When I first read *A Time of Gifts* I felt it in my *feet*. It spoke to my soles. It rang with what in German is called *Sehnsucht*: a yearning or wistful longing for the unknown and the mysterious. It made me want to stand up and march out – to walk into adventure. The book's strong magic derives in part from the atmosphere of miracle that attends Leigh Fermor's peregrinations. He strides with the seven-league boots of youth, fatigue barely registering as whole countries roll beneath his heel. The comforting rhythm of his journey – exertion, encounter, rest, food, sleep; exertion, encounter, rest, food, sleep – rocks its readers into feelings of happiness and invulnerability. *I could do this*, you think, *I could just start walking and keep going for a day or two, or three, or four, or more.*

Certainly, I have now walked hundreds of miles under Leigh Fermor's influence, and have carried his books for many of those miles, to read at the day's break or the day's end. One walk in particular was made directly as a result of Don's gift to me of *A Time of Gifts*. That walk happened in the December of 2007, a year when I was living and working back in Beijing. The city was a hard place to be that winter: the 2008 Olympics were imminent, and Beijing was convulsed by demolition and construction. *Hutongs* were being bulldozed by the hundred, compulsory purchase orders were being served on thousands of poorer homes, and dozens of new stadia and skyscrapers were being built. Migrant labourers toiled on the projects 24/7, in permanent halogen daylight, with massive speaker-banks blasting out Chinese radio to keep them entertained and educated as they did so.

I was stuck in the seventeenth-storey flat of an eighteen-storey building in a new development, from the windows of which I could count thirty-four cranes, each with a red PRC flag fluttering from its spire. My dawn chorus was the gong stroke of rivet on girder, the crump of the piston hammer, the high peal of hit steel. The notorious Beijing smog was choking, thickened by the cement dust raised by the construction. As soon as you stepped outside, you could feel the smog bite the throat and sting the eyes. When snow fell, it was grey. I read Leigh Fermor up in the flat, tried to look after my two young children adequately – and dreamed of getting out of the city and into clean air and white snow.

Then – as if Leigh Fermor himself had conjured it into being – an opportunity appeared: my friend Jon Miceler, a mountaineer and field conservationist, wrote inviting me to join him on a winter journey to the sacred 7,000-metre peak of Minya Konka, which rises between the Dadu and the Yalong rivers in Sichuan Province, south-west China.

I will never forget the days we subsequently spent up in the peaks of the Daxue range: the bright winter sun, the fearsome winter cold, the beaten-earth paths unfurling through oak-woods in the valleys, the high, snow-filled passes with their fluttering prayer flags and cairns of *mani* stones, and at last Minya Konka itself, a pyramidal mountain of exceptional beauty and danger, its flanks ribbed with huge snow flutes, its ridges running in fine lines up to its sharp summit . . .

I carried Leigh Fermor's *A Time of Gifts* with me throughout, and I brought the book safely back to sea level, too, its corners knackered from weeks in the rucksack and pannier, sand grains from a river beach stuck in its gutters, and a dried leaf of Himalayan oak tucked away between back page and back cover. I would later write about that journey in a walking book of my own called *The Old Ways*, in a chapter that is, I now see, unmistakably Leigh Fermorian in tone. His prose had inspired that journey on foot, and it shaped my subsequent account of it also; he had been my companion on the path, and he was my companion on the page, too. And Don's gift to me had continued to give, in ways neither of us could have foreseen.

*

Great art 'offers us images by which to imagine our lives', notes Lewis Hyde in his classic 1983 book, *The Gift*, '[and] once the imagination has been awakened it is procreative: through it we can give more than we were given, say more than we had to say'. This is a beautiful double-proposition: that art enlarges our repertoire for being, and that it further enables a giving *onwards* of that enriched utterance, that broadened perception.

I was given a copy of Hyde's *The Gift* – and I don't have that copy any longer, because I gave it to someone else, urging them to read it.

Gifts *give on*, says Hyde, this is their logic.
They are generous acts that incite generosity.
He contrasts two kinds of 'property': the
commodity and the gift. The commodity is
acquired and then hoarded, or resold. But the
gift is kept moving, given onwards in a new
form. Whereas the commodity circulates
according to the market economy (in which
relations are largely impersonal and conducted
with the aim of profiting the self), the gift
circulates according to the gift economy
(in which relations are largely personal and
conducted with the aim of profiting the other).
In the market economy, value accrues to the
individual by means of hoarding or 'saving'.
In the gift economy, value accrues between
individuals by means of giving and receiving.
This, for Hyde, is why gifts possess 'erotic life'
as property: when we give a gift, it is an erotic

act in the sense of *eros* as meaning 'attraction', 'union', a 'mutual involvement'.

Hyde is not to everyone's taste. I know economists who find him intolerably fey. His vision of a gift economy is appealing in theory, but not necessarily available to those locked into hardscrabble lives, gripped vice-tight by the cash economy. It is also hard to scale up gift economies from small groups to whole societies (though the Internet has made that much more possible since Hyde first wrote). And it's true that the evidence Hyde serves up in support of his gift thesis is a hell of a gumbo: superhero underwear, Scottish folk tales, Ezra Pound, Walt Whitman, the story of a couple who try to trade in their baby for a Corvette car . . . But to me at least, it mostly hangs together.

I am particularly moved by his deep interest

in what he calls 'the gift that, when it comes, speaks commandingly to the soul and irresistibly moves us'. The outcome of a gift is uncertain at the time of giving, but the fact that it *has been given* charges it with great potential to act upon the recipient for the good. Because of the gratitude we feel, and because the gift is by definition given freely, without obligation, we are encouraged to meet it with openness and with excitement. Unlike commodities, gifts -- in Hyde's account and my experience – possess an exceptional power to transform, to heal and to inspire.

That happened to me when Don gave me *A Time of Gifts*. It has happened to me numerous times, in fact – and it has almost always been the case that the gift which has spoken so 'commandingly' to my soul has been a printed book.

*

Not all books received as gifts are
transformative, of course. Sometimes the only
thing a book gives its reader is a paper cut.
I can't imagine having my soul spoken to by
John Prescott's biography, *Prezza* – though
this may be an indictment of my inner cynic,
rather than inarticulacy on the part of the
Mouth of the Humber.

But having been given so many astonishing
books over the years, I now in turn give away as
many books as I can. Birthdays, Christmases –
I give books, and pretty much only books, as
presents (always hard copies; I have never
given, or been given, an e-book). Once or
twice a year, I invite my students to my room
and let them take two or three books each from

several dozen that I've piled on the floor: the pleasure they take in choosing, and their disbelief that the books are *free*, reminds me of how precious books were to me when I was a student. Four years ago, I was given 200 or so books from the working library of my friend Roger Deakin, the great writer and environmentalist (*Waterlog*, *Wildwood*, *Notes from Walnut Tree Farm*), following his too-early death in 2006. Now I try to give individual books from that library to writers whose work I know Roger would have loved and wanted to encourage: I gave Roger's copy of Ted Hughes's *Wolfwatching*, for instance, to Rob Cowen, whose *Common Ground* is a wonderful hymn to a Harrogate edgeland and its inhabitants, and Roger's copy of Raymond Williams's *The Country and the City* to Melissa Harrison, whose novels and nature notes so

subtly break down the country/city opposition
that Williams also strove to erode.

There are five books that I give away again
and again, and they are among the books that
have struck me most forcefully. I try to make sure
that I always have several copies stockpiled,
ready to hand out. When I find a copy of one
of them in a bookshop, I buy it to add to the gift
pile, knowing that the right recipient will come
along sooner or later. The five books are Cormac
McCarthy's *Blood Meridian*, Vladimir Nabokov's
Lolita (care has to be taken with that one, I
admit), *A Time of Gifts* (of course), J. A. Baker's
The Peregrine and Nan Shepherd's *The Living
Mountain*, her slender masterpiece about the
Cairngorm mountains of north-east Scotland.
I'm not sure quite what that shortlist reveals of
my personality. I think perhaps I shouldn't
enquire too deeply.

Shepherd's is the book I have given away most often over the years. Forty copies? Fifty? I couldn't say. I once left a copy on a train, cursed when I realized I'd done so — then took comfort from the knowledge that a book lost by someone is often a book found by someone else (and hoped that Shepherd ended up in the hands of a reader rather than the bottom of a bin).

The giving-away of a copy of *The Living Mountain* that I remember most clearly happened in the Lairig Ghru in October 2013. The Lairig Ghru is the glacial valley that cuts through the Cairngorms from north to south. Where the path led through a steep-sided stream-cut, and crossed the water at a stepping-stone ford, I met a young man with a heavy pack. He had stopped to fill his flask and look at his map. We fell into conversation. He was called Samuel and he was from Singapore.

He spoke with distinctive fluency and candour.
He had come to the Highlands to escape some
kind of problem in his life, the nature of which
he did not specify. He was planning to spend
two nights out in the Cairngorms, though he
had no fixed idea of his route. I gave him some
advice about possible bothies he could stay in,
and wild-camping spots he could seek out –
and I also gave him the copy of *The Living
Mountain* that I had with me, hoping it might
keep him good company in hut or tent.

A week or so later, Samuel emailed:

After our meeting, my walk over the hills
of the Cairngorms took me the rest of the
day and proved to be the hardest thing
I had ever done. It was a most humbling
experience. Thank you, Robert, for sharing
Nan Shepherd's brilliant prose with me

and for giving me your copy of the book.
I started reading it on the train on my way
back to St Andrews, slowly, savouring each
word like honey. Every sentence was
poignant to a degree that I had never
experienced before. I wept as I read. Her
sensitivity to the land and its humble
creatures, humble forms, glorified through
her vision and thoughts, resonated deeply
with me. Thank you, thank you.

To receive such an open-hearted email was
itself a kind of gift, further proof of Hyde's
propositions that the gift can be transformative
and that the act of giving encourages the
onwards circulation of generosity. It reminded
me also of Shepherd's vision of nature itself as
abounding with gifts: offering wonders and
beauties but asking nothing of its recipients in

return. 'To see the Golden Eagle at close quarters,' she writes in *The Living Mountain*:

> requires knowledge and patience – though sometimes it may be a gift, as when once, just as I reached a summit cairn, an eagle rose from the far side of it and swept up in majestic circles above my head: I have never been nearer to the king of birds.

I recalled Nan's account of that 'gift' again last autumn, when I walked across the Cairngorms with my father, from Braemar to Tomintoul. We camped on the north- eastern shoulder of Ben Avon at around 3,000 feet, tucking our tents into the lee of a group of the granite tors that bulge from the plateau of that mountain. There we were sheltered from the big north-westerly wind that had buffeted us during the day. Just before dusk, Dad was in his tent and I was watching the sunset through the cleft between two tors. Suddenly a golden eagle came sailing past from the north, stiff-winged, its huge primaries trembling in the gale, passing perhaps thirty feet from me at its closest point. 'Dad! DAD! Get out here fast!' But by the time he was out of the tent the eagle was gone, lost in the corries to the west. 'Dad! You missed it! You won't believe it! A golden eagle just flew right past me!' And then, to our astonishment, another eagle appeared from the north, sailing past with stiff wings and trembling primaries, passing perhaps thirty feet from us at its closest point. Not one gift but two. *I have never been nearer to the king of birds . . .*

*

During the solitary months and years spent

writing a book, it can be easy to forget that it will – if you are lucky – live a social life: that your book might enter the imaginations and memories of its readers and thrive there, that your book might be crammed into pockets or backpacks and carried up mountains or to foreign countries, or that your book might be given by one person to another. Perhaps the aspect of authorship I cherish most are the glimpses I get of how my books are themselves carried, or are themselves given. When I sign books after readings, people frequently want their copies inscribed as gifts. *Would you make this out to my mother, who loves mountains? . . . to my brother, who lives in Calcutta? . . . to my best friend, who is ill? . . . to my father, who is no longer able to walk as far as he would wish . . . ?* Several times I've been asked to inscribe books to young children who can't yet read: *We want to give this book to them now, so it's waiting for them when they're ready for it.* These conversations with readers, and the stories that arise from them, are among the strongest of the forces that keep me writing.

As I work on this essay, over the Christmas of 2015, I know that a copy of my book *The Wild Places* is being sledge-hauled to the South Pole by a young Scottish adventurer called Luke Robertson, who is aiming to become the youngest Briton to ski there unassisted, unsupported and solo. Robertson's sledge weighs seventeen stone, and he is dragging it for thirty-five days over 730 miles of snow and ice, in temperatures as low as -50°C, and winds as high as 100mph. Under such circumstances every ounce counts, and I felt impossibly proud when I found out that *The Wild Places* (paperback weight: 8.9oz) had earned its place on his sledge, and impossibly excited at the thought of my sentences being read out there on the crystal continent, under the endless daylight of the austral summer.

*

This story began with the gift of a book, and it ends with one too. After three days away in Edinburgh, Don came back to Cambridge to stay with us for another couple of nights. The break had allowed me to catch up with work — and to get my priorities straight. I took two days off from the PhD, and Don and I *properly* walked and talked: out to Granchester along the river path, round the colleges, and from bookshop to bookshop. In G. David's I found a cut-price copy of Ezra Pound's *Selected Poems* from Faber, which includes his extraordinary versions of 'The River-Merchant's Wife: A

Letter', 'Song of the Bowmen of Shu', and Li Bai's poems of departure, including the 'Exile's Letter':

> And the wind lifting the song, and interrupting it,
> Tossing it up under the clouds.

> And all this comes to an end.
> And is not again to be met with.

I bought the book and gave it to Don as a farewell present. For two years or so afterwards, we wrote often and sent books to each other, back and forth over the Atlantic. Then one day Don wrote to say that he had been diagnosed with cancer, and that it had been caught late. He'd already begun chemotherapy. 'I have to go into this treatment room, Rob. I call it The Pain Room', he said.

'It's the worst place in the world.' I wrote more frequently, sent more books, sometimes two or three at a time. Don's replies slowed down, then stopped.

A year or so later, I got an email from an address I didn't recognize. It was from Don's daughter, Rachel, telling me that he had died. He had been glad to get the letters and books I had sent, she told me, even when he was no longer able to write back. 'Reading kept him alive,' she said, 'right till the end.'